Diacritics of Desire

Diacritics of Desire

Nikita Parik

HAWAKAL

Published by Hawakal Publishers
185 Kali Temple Road, Nimta, Kolkata 700049

Email: info@hawakal.com
Website: www.hawakal.com

First edition: April, 2019

Cover Art Illustration: Romain Lubière
Cover Art Concept: Bablu Goswami
Cover designed by Bitan Chakraborty

ISBN: 978-93-87883-56-7

Price: INR 299.00 | USD10.50

For
Mom and Dad
with all my love

Foreword

The proliferation of young and talented Indian poets writing in English in recent times is truly remarkable. It is as if the sluice gates have been raised and the literary landscape is awash with youthful poetry that proves beyond doubt that the English language in India is not just the language of communication and business, but that it can be the preferred language for creative composition, in almost any literary genre.

The thirty-four short poems in Nikita Parik's debut book of poems *Diacritics of Desire* exude exhilarating freshness, spontaneity and sincerity. The poems are finely wrought, fusing emotions, empathy, an enthusiastic passion for words, and a dedicated search for the *mot juste*.

In fact, Nikita Parik in her very first book of poems has traversed that extra mile by focusing on not just the impressionistic content but on the magic of words that creates a phonetic reverberation, so that even the familiar seems to bear an aura of mystery and mystique. The poems included in *Diacritics of Desire* are divided into two parts each part comprising seventeen short poems each. The arithmetical precision that is underpinned in the structure and arrangement of the titles of the poems in each part along with the glossary for ethnic terms and their culture-specific and region-specific meanings is noticeable. The words used in a few poems and explained in the glossary perhaps underscore that for Indians, using the English language for creative writing, is inevitably also a process of cultural translation.

Diacritics of Desire divided into two parts— *Semantics of Longing* and *Deixis of the Soil*- delves into the signs, symbols, and images of a collective culture and its subjective representation by the poetic persona. The crystallization of the trinity, ethos, pathos and logos are registered in poems as varied as the *Syntax of Thieving* and *My Mother Speaks Odiya*, or *Personal Pronouns* and *(Inter)stellar Gaze*.

In *The Heart of a Kalboishakh Sky* the ecstasy and agony of the poet's dilemma is conveyed powerfully-

The verses we compose in our
our slumber make love to
the ashes from yesterday's
cigarette, producing orgasms
like the ones we experience on
watching thunder tear open

the heart of a *kalboishakh* sky:

with you, everything is poetry, see?

The exploration and problematization of linguistic nuances through the utilization of signifiers such as "diacritics" and "deixis", along with the skilled and unusual use of "pixelated flowers", "alveolar sound" "mazuma" and "enjambment" among others set these poems apart, as wryly, the poet titles *"Phonetic Maze"* as the first poem in the volume. Phrases such as "seismic tsunami waves" or "thought-alligator" the latter reminiscent of Ted Hughes's poem *"Thought-fox"* bear the stamp of an intelligent and sensitive mind, in love with words and the world despite the occasional anxiety emanating from the challenges of life. Nikita Parik's poems will be appreciated by informed readers of poetry as her poems touch the hearts and minds of the readers due to her remarkable ability to infuse a subtle playfulness of words with multi-layered perspectives and poignancies.

Sanjukta Dasgupta
March 29, 2019

Introduction

The moment you begin to understand the secret tunes of the science behind languages, you can never go back to unobserving them in everyday life. If you are an artist, these ideas are bound to seep into the literature/art you create. I am grateful to the two years of my postgraduate degree in Linguistics at the University of Calcutta (87/1 College Street), for creating this precious linguistic consciousness by making me sit up and take heed of the magic with which languages affect us.

Diacritical marks, when attached to a letter, serve to change the sound value of that letter, and by logical extension, the word. With *Diacritics of Desire*, the intention was to create a meta-ish poetic collection, something which is in and of language; something which traverses the spectrum of varied emotions, sometimes with a linguistic looking-glass, be it the Semantics of Longing, or the more rooted emotions occupying the vowel-chasm between the soul and the soil. The result is this oddball word-mixture of nouns and pronouns in rustic mother tongues, the secret chanting of old magic practiced by grandmothers, the language of our relationship with our bodies, and the language of prayers and politics.

I think the best way to read a collection of poems is in lento mode- you have to read one poem several times, taste its essence- first slowly, then wolfishly-, let it occupy every fibre of your being, and then revel in the after-taste. If you take away even a single idea, sound, phrase, or line from this book, I'll consider this book a success.

Nikita Parik,
March 31st, 2019
Hyderabad

Acknowledgements

To my family, for everything words cannot express. I love you all, so very much, no matter which bit of the globe you inhabit. You make me who I am.

To The Fox Poetry Box and its curator Tricia Marcella Cimera for displaying my poem *'My Mother Speaks Odiya'* in the box in January 2019. The Fox Poetry Box, an actual poetry box located in St. Charles Illinois, is a part of the Poetry in Public Spaces movement.

Gratitude also goes to the following journals and their poetry editors for publishing some of the poems (some rechristened) that appear in this collection:

The Metaworker (*'A Russian Romance'*), Aainanagar (*'Gaach-Tawla'* and *'The Heart of a Kalboishakh Sky'*), The Bombay Literary Magazine (*'First Names Matter'*, forthcoming), The First Anthology of World Gogyoshi (*'Orange Origami'*)

To Mr. Sanjeev Sethi, for being the Professor Dumbledore to my Harry Potter. This book simply would not have seen the light of the day had you not believed in my poetry. You sharpen my poetic instincts. I learn so much from you with every interaction. For your patience, guidance, efforts, humility, and faith, thank you. Also, thank you for believing in this collection enough to write the blurb for it.

To Padma Shri Keki Daruwala, for patiently reading through the poems and writing the blurb for the collection despite an opposing personal resolution for the year ("no blurbs, more herbs"). I am eternally thankful to you.

To Professor Sanjukta Dasgupta ma'am, for being generous enough to write the foreword for this collection. Your belief in me makes me believe in myself better.

I am extremely thankful to my friends Romain Lubière, for the cover art illustration, and Bablu Goswami, for the cover art concept. La couverture est parfaite, je suis très reconnaissant. Je vous aime tous les deux immensément. Le dernier poème de cette collection, *'Call From Saint Etienne'*, fût inspiré à la suite d'un appel video avec M. Goswami.

To Adarsh Yagnik, for being my favourite muse and, more importantly, a once-in-a-lifetime kind of a friend. Thank you for always inspiring the best in me.

To Michelle D'costa, Arjun Rajendran, Nabina Das, and Mihir Vatsa, for your kindness and unwavering love for the craft, thank you.

To Amit Shankar Saha, for having an eye for even the sneakiest of typos, and a heart that is so selfless and dedicated to literature. To Sufia Khatoon and Jagari Mukherjee, for all the literary discussions late into the night, and so much more.

To *Rhythm Divine Poets*, for creating the constant safespace of poetry in our lives.

And last but not the least, love and gratitude to *Hawakal Publishers*.

"You're rowing by wordlight"
Paul Célan

CONTENTS

Semantics of Longing

Deixis of the Soil

Semantics of Longing

Phonetic Maze

Our liquid existences
intersect at

an incidental point
in a wave universe.

Words act as lithe
talismans to

the portals of your
fluid identities. I'm

a traveler forever lost
in your *wordways*.

Syntax of Thieving

This poem is an act of theft.
If you dip into it, you will

see how these lines have looted
memory lockers to the last mazuma.

This poem is an exercise in shop-
lifting. It extols the personal

without permission. See how
the enjambments display

lines of your laughter. These
verses are an exploit in burglary.

The rhythms chip at your ruins,
the words pilferage from your pilgrim,

the sounds hijack your sentience only
to make poems out of it. If you know

where to look, you may meet yourself
at a soundsquare near line 16.

This is an act of theft,
but so are all things love.

22

Hexed

Our rituals have their own
grammar. The language

of longing invokes a charm
and spell they call poetry.

In between cycles of Alt-Rock
and Soul, it lights candles

of meaning from the fire
of my shamanistic being:

The circle is complete. The
goddess has found herself.

A Russian Romance

One fanciful Calcutta summer,
world maps were ripped off
from overused geography textbooks
in an act of innocent revolution.

You cherry-picked ecstatic reds
from sunsetty Russian sky-palettes,
scooping the colors out of glossy
pages, and blending them expertly with

the flirty blues of river Moskva.
I, too, borrowed the antique
old world hues of St. Basil's cathedral
from a sparkling summer's day,

and together, you and I,
we finger-painted the streets of Calcutta
with the colors of our Revolution.

Diacritics of Desire

My French teacher draws
a tailed-c -(ç)- in class, "a cédille",
she says, and in my head, I

first link cédille with *dil*- heart-
then *dil* with its French
twin - 'le *coeur*. A cédille,
she explains, softens the harshness
of sounds. A *dil,* however
eats softnesses for breakfast. A *dil is*

blood, flesh, muscle, bone,
and some *jigar*-
a ruin in rawness that only knows
the language of fierce love
and aggressive prayers while
it loves and loves before splintering
in the flood of its bruises.

A cédille, she points, births soft
[C]s and eliminates
the rough [K]s in the French language,
but then, why doesn't it save the French

25

heart from the same brassiness?
why is the c in *'coeur'* still harsh
in this tongue,

if not by the design of desire?

The Heart of a *Kalboishakh* Sky

(i)
On no-heartbeat-days as these,
we'd just lie here, next to
our aborted nothingness,
watching their crimson corpses decay,
and bleedbleedbleed it out
in the name of creativity.

(ii)
I secretly believe still
that rain has a memory,
and that I am its memory mirror,
but the reflections are too obscure,
too disparate, you see,
to be strung together in
words or images.

(iii)
The verses we compose in our
our slumber make love to
the ashes from yesterday's
cigarette, producing orgasms
like the ones we experience on
watching thunder tear open
the heart of a *kalboishakh* sky:

with you, everything is poetry, see?

27

À La Carte

Menu is the same since the last decade.

For starters my favorite jazz songs you
would bob your head to while working
late. A plate of warm nostalgia to increase
the appetite for genuine smiles (rarity in your
city). For the main course, Philosophy
served with the right garnish (it's Levi-
Strauss today, but I know you enjoy Nietzsche
and Foucault more). Next, *kulhads* of tea-
memories to wash it all down. Dessert?
Sicksweet poems on a flatscreen.

Now the meal is tepid. I hear your preferences
are changing.

Gaach Tawla

On red-eyed university summers,
broken *Radhachura* petals from that lane
overlooking Centenary Building fly
across guilty noon-naps, phosphenous
blindness, and their dull fated
 in-between-ness,

much like half-baked poems
scurrying in and out of
consciousness,

before being lulled by passive joint
fumes into drowsy summer dreams where
their yellowness makes hot, hot love
to a sea of yellow taxis and cheap
second-hand book covers
outside dusty-magical bookstores.

On such passively pretty university
summers, when the world stands still,

I wonder if you will remember
say, twenty years hence,

that *kalboishakh* from years ago
when, at *Maidan*, we'd smoked one
together in turns, my first,
and the world had stood still.

Couloirs of Want

Jugni finds herself in the heart of
Chandigarh's
sector satrah, the green fire of her
being gently
stroked by the *Lohri* air, the embrace of
the *rang-dariya*

warming all winters. *Jugni* floats
amidst
women selling trinkets, *jhumkas*
and *parandis* and embellished
dupattas in
the brightest fabrics. *Jugni* sees

herself in a hundred glass reflections,
in the eyelinered-
irises of all those women, in
the collective
khanak of their glass- bangles as they
go about their
businesses, in the soft lilts of their
Punjabi-Hindi

bargaining skills. *Jugni*
exudes *Rangreza*'s physical
absence, perpetually existing in
the vowel-chasm between
jugni and *jogan*

(Inter)stellar Gaze

Since tonight I am hopelessly in love
with you, I dream of Sagan. If we

are indeed the universe experiencing
itself, it is safe to say your molten

black gaze contains universes of
universes that explode *star stuff*

whenever they meet the fulminating
thunders in mine. Tonight, the star-

crossed pathways forget all laws of
physics, as they gravitate towards

those two contemplating black holes
of wondrous, cerebral desires.

Nursery

*"Aur bhi gham hai zamane me
mohabbat k siwa"*
~ Faiz Ahmed Faiz

(i)
The pixelated flowers
from

an almost-decade
timestamp

still smell of freshly-
dug

earth- *gili mitti*- in
my

cobble-stoned amygdalan
crevices.

(ii)
We grow old. You ask
what I feel

34

about emotions not
 mattering. I say

something smart. That
night,

Faiz visits my thought-garden,
and

together, we water flowers.

Apraxia

This waiting is charred skin, its scar,
a permanence in epidermal memory.

This waiting is the echo of silent, hot
venom in neuron synapses, it seethes

and stings unreliably. This waiting is
a thought-alligator that bites off my

tongue and feeds on my language in
loud chomps. This waiting erupts

as seismic tsunami waves in my
numberless nerves, demolishing

some quiddities. This waiting is
the disease and the diseased. This

waiting is the cage and the caged,
and I wouldn't have it any other way.

First Names Matter

(i)
At an almost-dawn one February, I
tell you how my parents had
almost named me after a
Mahadevi Verma poetry
collection
(twice)

निहार(इका)। नीरजा

before the Russians
invaded the familial
decision-making, and
I was christened

Никита | Nikita

*"Funny how poetry finds
ways of coming back"*, I chime.

(ii)
Like Gulzar and so many
others, I want to write

a poem on that precise
moment when one falls in
love with their first names for
the first time as I

imagine the syllables
forming in your mouth-
the nasal n rushing into
the voiceless velar stop,
both holding on to the long ē
that shapes your lips into
the ghost of a smile, ending
in the hushed softness of
an alveolar sound:

निकिता

But you only ever address
me with 'you' in its various
shades, using the elusiveness
of language to your advantage.

'Names don't matter', you decide.

Afterglow

(i)
I build on our discussion
where
we'd toyed with the possibility

of someone trying to trace our
legacies
someday- unexpectedly- like

a lover tailing the back-
bone
of a new love in the dark.

(ii)
They say some of my prettiest
poems
are the ones that dance to your
dicta. I

smile, bottle your fragrance, dip my
pen in it,
and create a picture-gallery of pretty ink
engravings.

(iii)
When my tracer looks for
me in my
language, what if my breathless-
ness is eclipsed

on the cave of your
anatomy; my gaze, intangible,
lost in your
well-written, galactic pupils;

me, a non-entity against
your repetitive,
linguistic presence? What if,
 in the *afterglow*

of my *wordlight*, the letters
that paint you
luminesce brighter than my
own name?

The Eye of Language

(i)
Barb wires of an infinite
linguistic cosmos
tongue and untongue
the cerebration of my
minus-male existence, till
I hold them by the thorns
and blood-kiss them.

(ii)
How we speak
isn't very different
from how we listen,
and how we love.

(iii)
Unlike you, my unphallic
language diffuses
love evenly all over
the body rather than being
fixated on singularities.
Its sounds penetrate the hollows

between fingers, the bend
of the nape, the caves
of your ears, and the hulls
below the eyes
with equal affection.

(iv)
How we Love
isn't very different
from how we listen
and how we speak.

Semantics of Longing

The brown *neem*
leaves lap the past in their
veins, the red ones
sprout present from
where the old
ones left

               and before we know it, I,
           75, am watering purple petunias
         by blue mountain shadows. Having
             forgotten the semantics
              of longing, I create new
        glossaries inked in blue sunlight,

and mark them with the dust of
butterfly wings. My solitude tends
to a library in the hills,
something you always wanted,
 but we do not know
 each other anymore.

43

You, 76, with amnesia
easing the grief in your
gullet, look at life so
differently now. Perhaps

you still drink
could-have-beens with your
sundowner, only, it feels
new every day. On some days,
you indistinctly remember

that young girl
with sparrows in her
hair who used to write
poems after poems
about your eyes.

Unlearning the Grammar of Love

I unteach myself
the subtle semantics
of longing.

Unlearn the inflections
of my navel's nervous
fluttering.

Unremember imagined
affixes of your treasured
companionship.

Unlayer the configurations
of instincts and emotions
from my being.

Undo everything every couple
of years, like a ritual
in nullity.

Unloving you is the art
I forget and master
concomitantly.

Deixis of the Soil

Mother Tongue

If you plan to rule over
a people, material imperialism
is never enough.

You must take hold of
the language,
seize its sounds,

cause them to choke
in the very throats
they originate from.

Next, you must strip it
naked, cause shame to
the tongues that speak it.

Then, to be really sure,
plant the seeds of doubt
carefully, and when the brains

begin to question
the very tenets of
the *uncivilized truths*

of a once-enslaved language,
give yourself a pat and
consider your job done well.

Salat
(*For Zarin Nisa*)

Magrib Azan spreads through
the inverted cosmos of

your dark pupils, stumbling into
sounds in today's memory:

Fajr, Zohar, Asar. Allah'u'akbar(s)
compound in sunlit mind crevices,

then gush out as your ricocheting
laughter. Evenings such as these

weave faith out of air, words out of
light, and vision out of

nothingness: *Zarin Nisa, look*
how you convert
kafirs into believers.

Important Nouns, Circa 1944

When grandfather had migrated to Bengal
 as a lad of sixteen, he was unaware of
a number of things. *One*, he hardly knew that he
would never go back to that *dhani* in
Shekhawati again where all sunsets spelled
'familiarity' and each syllable in the local tongue
 hollered 'home'.

Two, that he would never see those sand
dunes again where he used to play
hide and seek till the last of the northern sun
decamped, always losing a *mojari* or two which
were mysteriously never found again.

Three, that never again
 would he hear the familiar grunt of camels
that lazed outside every third *kothi* of
that lost neighborhood where the owners
 let them pet and play with one
as long as they wanted.

Four, that *'home'* isn't always where the heart is;
nobody wishes to leave *home* unless *'home'*

51

itself wishes them out in an act of tough love.

Five, that for some, home is where
 they must go in search of *survival,*
subsistence, and similar hefty nouns

Personal Pronouns, circa 2014

(i)
The summer I first visited the home-state
 of my ancestors, cultural appropriation died
 a disappointed death beside a car window.
It ghosted into a blank expression on my face
 at the non-existent sand dunes, indigenous people,
and other lies one learns from popular culture. Instead,
what stood before me was tall malls, showrooms,
and 'regular' (?) people laughing, talking
and moving around the pretty pink city.

(ii)
(I was born just weeks after my city had bid a teary-
eyed farewell to Dugga Ma, *with* 'asche bochor abar hobe'
reverberating in every para. *This city was the only one I*
 had carried in my heart for twenty- one *years, the only one*
I had nurtured, loved, and hated like a part of myself).

(iii)
That summer, I discovered that it is quite alright
to have two *homes,* even though you feel a little
alien to both- to the *former,* by *origin,*
to the *latter,* by *habits.*

It is okay to spoon a mother tongue after
twenty-one years of existence-
 to be awkward in a language that *ought to be*
yours, but feels familiarly distant -the retroflex sounds
getting stuck in your throat.
 It is okay as long as the nasal 'M' in their
'Padharo 'M'hare Des' quietly morphs into
an alveolar 'T', and their personal pronouns
warmly becomes yours.

Coldnoon Winters, Late 90s

Back in those days, the household used to be
perpetually fragrant, the *verandahs* proudly displaying
 various assortments of *saag* and other edibles-

sangri, phali, kaachra, podina, papad, mangori- all
meticulously kept in separate *daliyas*
to dry in the winter sun. Sometimes various recipes

of *achaars* and *murabbas* would grab our attention.
Grandmother, always clad in cotton *leheriya* sarees
and smelling of maternal love, would

chide us- asking us to practice '*thyavas*' – restraint-,
 not to spoil the efforts, to go
outside and play instead. Disappointed, I would sneak

up to the boundary-less roof next to you sprawled
on a straw mattress, snug in your black shawl, emanating
the familiar curious aroma of coconut oil,

tobacco, and talcum. On those coldnoon winters,
covering my face with your shawl, I would
experience a thousand lifetimes through your stories.

Panchkutta

Thar sun- arrogant warrior that
exterminated all vegetation in the *marubhumi,*
merciful only to cactus, weed, and wild berries

Wild berries and weed- staple natives put
on their plates night after night; survival in *registaan*
was a song sung through the lips of deprivation.

Deprivation drew power when one day the natives
assembled the discarded weeds and seeds
together- slender *sangri* , bitter *kair,* wild

wild *kumatiya* seeds, *gunda* berries, stinging
mathani mirch- and cooked them all together
in mustard oil and spices, creating 'panchakutta' curry

Deprivation and discardment become power
and sustenance when the oppressed and rejected
come together to create their own tunes of survival

Orange Origami

Summers in sun-stung Thar crumple
into an icy moon over Pushkar's Ink-spilled
skies, then transmorph into the stillness of
Aravalli extensions: Papa, you are the anchor
to this soul's histories and geographies.

My Mother Speaks Odiya

In brief moments of complex linguistic
exchanges, the water-fetchers from the sea-state
of Odisha connect to my mother
in a way I never could.

The mutual pleasantries shared taste like
sea-salt on the tongue, the phrases vibrant, like
conch shells buried under the tides
of a shared history in a shared land.

Oh how now the rhythmic, chant-like banter
shape-shifts before my eyes into frothy saltsprays, now
Rathyatra-chaos, now rushed rustic
banter in breezy paddy fields!

Every time my mother speaks Odiya, she exposes me
to a history- latent, unexplored- and in its lilts
I imagine the lulls of a sleeping sea,
the sounds- all its phones and morphs-

transporting me to another time, in another state,
where the colors of the sky write themselves over
the playfully turbulent seas in
the same rhythms and cadences.

Inheritance

Grandma often sat me down,
eyed me with a concern that
only foremothers carry in
their blood- its shadow
bubbling through the lines
on her face- then fisted

dried red chillies, rock salt,
and mustard seeds with
the age-old magic of
womanhood and blood ties.
Incense fumes and secret
chants were sewn
into two rotations
clockwise, and one
anti-clockwise
before the *nazar* was sucked
into the magic mix,

which was then left to burn
on a blue-orange flame.
'If the chillies don't
burn your eyes, it means

you had the buri drishti ", she
would explain.

With grandma gone,
mother has taken it upon
herself to remove my evil
eye on certain Saturdays.
I often fear that

this talisman of love
is the inheritance I
will never bequeath.

Mothering

(i)
In my native language, we have
multitudinous

mothers- mothering being more of an
aesthetic

than a biological role.
So you, like every other *Rajasthani*

grandmother,
were '*ma*' for all subsequent generations.

(ii)
If motherhood had a sound, it
would be a mixed tape

of your high-pitched *bhajans* in my
burnt orange subconscious,

the *swoosh* of your orange-*paar*
cotton sarees, the soft grace

of your muted steps, and an echo of
your summons

in dusty village rooms.

(iii)
Haven't you heard, ma?

Your death has also orphaned

the loft of pigeons, the scurry of

squirrels, and all the inhabitants

of the old Neem tree.

Living Room

The stilettos are discarded
at the porch,
bra unhooked with the next
bare steps,
its left strap held delicately
between
the thumb and index fingers
before being slid
down a shoulder and pulled
out from under
the shirt's sleeve, like a painter's
final stroke over
a pigmented masterpiece.

A whiff of the musk before
it is discarded into the dark.
Lung-fulls of liquid home
rush in to occupy the city
underneath the flesh.

Every loose curl over
the plaid-shirt, then,
is checked into a

bun, while the stereo
blurs *time* and
timeless,
and a bookmarked page
begins to burn.

Kitchen

Some blue-grey noons
find her glorious mess
content, almost meditative,
behind the kitchen counter.

Old T-shirt, a gallimaufry
of flavors, textures, shades,
curls aromatic from
heady fumes, nape
bobbing to a random
guitar solo, thighs sweaty
from all the dancing,
senses blissfully
unaware of the diluting
 evening sun.

Freedom on such noons
is not knowing coriander
from cumin, but relying
on aromas while choosing
the spice

Roof

Winter sun drinks from
her shoulder moles as she
waters the flora which
lines the roof boundary
like lost lovers-

Aloe-Vera, Tulsi, Marigold,
Hibiscus, a creeper or two,
Rajanigandha. Like a ritualistic
exercise in misplaced affection,
organic vegetable waste is fed
to the soil.

Saree tucked away, out of
habit, manure thrown lovingly
into the pot, fingernails dug deep
into the cool, wet mud, senses
playing with the earthiness-

Some mud find shelter
in the tenderness underneath
those elongated nails.

A sneaky caterpillar crawls down
the softness of the nape, down
the shoulder blades, towards
that mole unseen.

Crow's Feet

A silly punchline,
my sideways glance:
a *tabassum* travels

up your face,
through the chasms of
your *chashm*,

branching out
from underneath, like
Darya-e-Sindh's outspread

tributaries. It cuts
through your skin,
carving repositories

of unrestrained
elation. A single strand
of hair arrests time.

The humor
is lost on me

The Thirsting Hollow

of art paper
begins to store
globules of color

into its navel. *Zarin*
smears the *Golden*
in a Persian irony of

naming. The pigmented
brush is soused in
cyan liquid before it

charters chrysoprase
green on periwinkle blue.
The swooshing brush-

strokes 'gainst paper, then,
mark jets of gold against
lush black outlines. *Zarin Nisa,*

how you make
the painting come alive
with a smile!

Coloring

Blood clots from
needle invasions mark
your hands with
blue lines that resemble

secret maps to
prohibited places. They
take me on a voyage to
a pastness where

the only blue lines were
on a virtual map, depicting
the journey of Nile
around the calendar.

In my dreams
blue lines criss-cross our
conversations, & Geography-
History text-books. You had

once told me
of your trip to Puri beach
as a twenty-something

some forty years ago. How

the sea had reflected
your thrill of freedom. "*We
must visit Puri together*", you'd
insisted. The hospital room

in the present is blue
and your eyes
don't recognize me.

Call from Saint Étienne

It's been months since your last
call. You reminisce about that trip
to the Alps with a group of kind
strangers. Of course I know
the story by heart. I remind you
of your casual drinking that
night which had led to stranger actions.
You laugh. The talk shifts
to your recent trip to Bari in Italy. You
say how your days began with
beer and crépes, leading to
museum hunts and art exhibits. How
you let waiters choose the menu,
just for the thrill of it. I imagine
the city to be full of laughter
and sunshine. We must dance
when I visit next, you say. And drink,
I add. Yes, you concede. Drinking
is important. Or maybe, you interject,
travel to some place together. I make
 plans in my mind. This and that, and
some more. It's not wise, you
say, to talk about depression at 28. Or

loneliness, for that matter. I wonder
if you wanted to begin the call with
this statement. It's not okay, you insist,
to call your friends and tell them
about the hollowness in your heart.
I think my mother is calling me
for dinner.

GLOSARRY

Cédille - A hook-like diacritical mark under the letter C in the French language that functions to alter pronunciation

Dil- 'Heart' in the Hindi language

Le Coeur- 'The Heart' in the French Language

Jigar- Literal meanings: Liver in Hindi, Slang for 'friend' in Urdu/Persian. On a metaphorical level, it stands for courage and love.

Kalboishakh- Nor'westers

Radhachura- A kind of bright yellow flower

Maidan- An open space in or near a town; in this poem, it refers to a vast stretch of land known by the same name in central Kolkata

Jugni- From Punjabi Folklore: **"Jugni** is an age-old narrative device used in Punjabi Folk Music and sung at Punjabi weddings in India, Pakistan, US, Canada, Australia and UK. The word literally means 'Female Firefly', in folk music it stands in for the poet-writer who uses Jugni as an innocent observer to make incisive, often humorous, and sometimes sad but always touching observations. In spiritual poetry, Jugni means the spirit of life, or essence of life."

Sector satrah- sector 17

Lohri- A midwinter festival primarily celebrated in and around the Indian state of Punjab to celebrate the winter solstice.

Rang Dariya- A Stream of color

Jhumkas- Earrings

Parandi- A type of hair accessory worn by women in the Indian state of Punjab

Dupattas- Indian Scarf

Khanak- Chime of Bangles

Rangrez- Persian word meaning 'dyer'; widely used in Persian poetry (Refer to Rang-Dariya above)

Jogan- Female ascetic (*Jogi-Jogan*)

Aur Bhi Gham Hai Zamane Me Mohabbat Ke Siwa- There are other pains in life too other than the one that love entails.

Salat- The ritual prayer of Muslims, performed 5 times a day. A *muezzin* calls out the *azaan* (prayer-call) five times a day to summon the worshippers. These prayers are *Fazr, Zohar, Asar, Maghrib*, and *Isha*.

Dhani- Kind of hamlet found in sandy regions in states like Rajasthan

Shekhawati- A region located in the north-eastern part of Rajasthan

Mojari- Type of handcrafted footwear worn by locals for centuries in states like Rajasthan

Kothi- Houses

Dugga Ma- Goddess Durga

Asche bochor abar hobe- Until next year (language: Bangla)- chanted while bidding farewell to Goddess Durga during the festival of Durga Puja.

Para- Neighbourhood/society

Padharo 'M'hare Des - Welcome to our land" (language: Marwadi)

Saag- vegetables

Daliyas- Baskets

Achaars- Salty pickles

Murabbas- Sweetened pickles

Leheriya sarees- A traditional style of tie and dye practiced in Rajasthan. *Leheriya* sarees are brightly colored and have distinctive patterns.

Thyavas- Restraint

Marubhumi- Desert

Registaan- Desert

Nazar- Evil eye

Buri Drishti- Evil eye

Bhajans- Prayers

Paar- The border of a Saree

Tabassum- Smile

Chashm- Eyes

Darya-E-Sindh- Alternatively also known as the Indus River